Living the Beatitudes: Daily Reflections for Lent

From the L'Arche Daybreak Community

Foreword by Henri J. M. Nouwen

ST.
ANTHONY
MESSENGER
PRESS

Cincinnati, Ohio

Scripture quotations are from the *New Revised Standard Version of the Bible*, copyright ©1989 by the Division of Christian Education of the National Council of Churches of Christ in the U.S.A. Used by permission. All rights reserved.

Cover design by Leslie Brod
Book design by Julie Lonneman

ISBN 0-86716-231-7

Published by St. Anthony Messenger Press
Printed in the U.S.A.

Contents

Acknowledgments

The following people from the L'Arche Daybreak Community in Toronto, Canada, compiled the material for this book: Henri J. M. Nouwen, pastor of L'Arche Daybreak—foreword; Gordon Henry, Daybreak pastoral team and life member—editorial advisor; Peter Doll, assistant—photographs; Paula Keleher, assistant—photographs; Gail Stevens, assistant—introduction, computer manager; Brad Colby, assistant—weekly reflections; Sue Mosteller, assistant—daily reflections.

We are also grateful to those people who have allowed us to publish their photographs, illustrations and stories. Without them this book would not have been possible: Claudia, Raphael, Lynn, Roy, Ronnie, Thelis, Michael A., Rex, Jeanne, Helen H., Loretta, Marcie, Peter R., David G., Annie, Peggy, Joanne, Monica Anne's parents, Janice, Bill, Janet, Hsi Fu, Peter P., Patsy, Patrick, Mary B., Mary Anne, Doug, Tracy, Julie, Trevor, Mel, Patrick, Carol, Gordon H., Greg, Karen, Kathy, Timmy, Gordon F., George, Anne Marie, Ellen, David H., Mary Bee, Carl, Heather, Andy, Joe, Wendy, John S., Rosie, Clara, Elizabeth, Alia, Suzanne, Linda, Ian, Cheryl, Margaret, Mary and Joe, Annie, Jane, Helen F., Lloyd, Francis, Michael R., Sean, Michael B., Adam, Carmen, John B., Helen J., Tony, Stephanie.

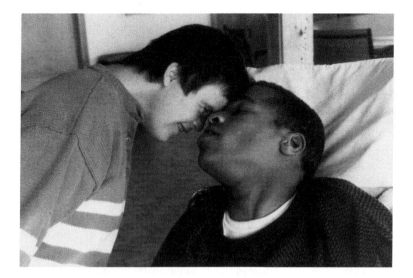

Foreword

This Lenten book was born in a community of people who have mental handicaps. The community, called "L'Arche Daybreak," is located in Toronto, Canada. I have lived there for nearly eight years and have come to think of it as my home. Although L'Arche Daybreak is rather large—fifty people with mental handicaps and close to sixty assistants who live with them—and although L'Arche Daybreak consists of more than eleven homes spread out over the greater Toronto area with people constantly coming and going, I have found it to be a welcoming, safe, life-giving place. It is a place where people who in our society are considered marginal offer me a home and keep me focused on what is essential in life: God, people—and love.

A few years ago we composed our own Lenten book, with reflections by and about our own community members. We decided to use the Beatitudes as the structure of the book and the basis of the daily reflections. We included drawings made by the members with disabilities and their assistants, photographs from our many albums and colored sheets of hearts to cut out. The book that emerged was by the community and for the community.

As we used our Lenten book we discovered its magic: Simple, direct, down-to-earth, it was not only a popular book, but an effective tool to prepare ourselves for Easter. As we read the words written by our own people, and as we wrote the names of those we wanted to pray for on the cutout hearts, we became aware that we ourselves—little and often very weak people—are indeed God's people journeying to the promised land. Through our Lenten book we discovered who we are in God's eyes: chosen, blessed and broken children of God called to give ourselves to others as a source of hope.

As the L'Arche Daybreak community enters its twenty-fifth year, we ask, "What do we have to offer to those who do not belong to our community but who share our hopes and dreams?" Sister Sue Mosteller, a longtime member of Daybreak, suggested that one thing we have to offer is our Lenten book. Our community is a microcosm of the world around us. We are handicapped and able-minded people. We are married and single people. We are Christians, Jews, Moslems and Buddhists. We are black and white and brown people. We are people from ten different nationalities and three different continents. We are children and adults, young and old people. But, most of all, we are people who share in the joys and the pains of all "little people" in the world.

At Sue's suggestion, then, we offer our Lenten book to all the "little" people, to that worldwide community of women, men and children who are together trying to move from a life in bondage to the powers of darkness to a life as children of the light.

We are especially thinking of families and communities who want to pray together without excluding anyone. So often children feel that the prayers said at table are for adults only, or adults feel that some prayers are just for kids. Some people around the table feel excluded because of their special circumstances. We wanted to offer a way of praying that gives something simple to read, something simple to see and something simple to do, so that everyone can take part.

I would like to offer a few thoughts that might help you and others to use this book as well as possible.

All of us, whether rich or poor, powerful or powerless, are

"little" people because we are God's children who need desperately to be loved. The littlest among us help us to pray because they are least tempted to show off before God. They know that God does not need words or pictures or actions to understand our needs. God knows what we need and wants only an open heart that reaches out for love.

One member of our community has a limited vocabulary, but the words he knows best are *open heart*. Whenever he prays for others he says: "I pray that you have an open heart." Those who hear his prayer are always deeply touched because it summarizes all we can ask for.

God's blessing is hidden in our littleness like a diamond in its setting. That is why Jesus said "Blessed are the poor" and "Blessed are those who mourn." Precisely where we cannot help ourselves, where we are poor and cry, the gifts of love, joy, peace and simple trust are held. Jesus did not say "Blessed are those who care for the poor" or "Blessed are those who console the mourners," because caring and consoling often happen from a place of strength, whereas God's blessing emerges from weakness. Just as God's love is revealed to us by Jesus coming among us in weakness, so too are God's blessings given to us through those whom the world considers little, poor, weak, useless or marginal.

By placing the little ones among us in the center of our prayer life, this Lenten book becomes a book of special blessings. In one of our Daybreak houses lives Janice. She cannot speak and needs full-time care to live well. But she can walk, and she puts on the wall the cutout hearts with the names of those for whom we want to pray. She does this with great enthusiasm and fervor every day of Lent. Thus she blesses all around the table in a special way.

But there is more. All of us are not only little but also great. God has looked with mercy on our littleness and has made us sons and daughters of the Most High, people with the unique vocation to announce good news to the poor and liberate the captives.

In our littleness we discover our wholeness; in our sickness we realize our joy; in the confession of our sin we come to see grace. Our littleness allows us to claim our greatness before God.

This Lenten book is for little people, not to make them feel little, but to help them realize that they are the ones who shape God's Kingdom and are the source of hope for our world. All the saints in the history of humanity were little people who claimed their greatness before God, a greatness based not on success, power and influence but on love that is stronger than death.

I have been increasingly amazed since coming to Daybreak how people with mental disabilities can become the "professors" in God's Kingdom. They teach more about forgiveness, hospitality, kindness, perseverance and, most of all, love than any school of theology. They lead us directly to the heart of God.

What is true for people with mental disabilities is true for anyone who is poor in spirit. Every time we recognize our own poverty of spirit, whether as children who feel insecure, or as parents who worry about the future, or as single people who search for a place in life, we are challenged to claim the Kingdom as our inheritance.

Through using this Lenten book you will come to realize that living the Beatitudes is indeed living as the chosen people of God. We can walk through our violent and fear-filled world with heads erect, confident that God is our guide and will fulfill the deepest desires of our hearts. As you write on the cutout hearts the names of the many people you think of and care for, you will come to see the Kingdom of God among you. It is a kingdom of suffering people, but also a kingdom of joy and peace.

I truly hope and pray that this Lenten book will be a source of life for you, your family and your friends. When you have guests around your table, guests who just happen to drop in for a meal or guests who come to stay with you for a while, I can assure you that they will feel drawn into the circle of love that this book helps to create. They will have a glimpse of the Kingdom as they become part of your prayers. You might think that these prayers are insignificant, and you might even feel a little embarrassed praying them in the presence of those you do not know well, but trust that the resurrection you are waiting for is already happening—within you and within all who join you in prayer.

—Henri J. M. Nouwen
Pastor, L'Arche Daybreak

Introduction

The Stephenson House Experience

Each evening Helen clears the dishes from the table and returns to her seat. John finds a candle, lights it and puts it at his place until we gently remind him to move it to the center of the table where we can all enjoy it. Ronnie goes over to the wall switch to turn down the lights. The person who cooked dinner that night leads the prayer, beginning by reading the beatitude for the day. We take a few moments of silence to think about what was just read. Then Claudia picks up her guitar and starts gently strumming a song; we begin singing as we recognize the melody.

Someone reads the reflection for the day, and we take time to talk about what touched us as we heard the story. If the message is about loneliness, someone might ask, "Have there ever been times when you've felt alone? Why? What could you do to help someone who is lonely to feel better? Could we pray for someone you know who seems lonely?"

Next we choose a paper heart to carry our prayer requests. We pass the heart and pen around the table, and each person writes on the heart the name of someone or something for which they wish to pray. We help John spell out the letters of the names he wants to include. Helen doesn't verbalize her thoughts, so a buddy will talk with her about the people she would like to include in her prayers and the buddy then writes down those names. By the time the heart has circled the table, it is full of intentions we want to bring to God that evening. We then spend several quiet moments together. Those who want to say anything during this time share their thoughts. We finish by holding hands and saying the Lord's Prayer together.

At this point Claudia picks up the guitar again, and we sing several songs we really enjoy. During this time Michael will attach the heart to our Lenten poster. Through the week, the hearts form a circle around the picture we chose to represent the week's beatitude.

Then when the singing is finished, there is a rush to see who can blow out the candle. We head out to do the dishes, and catch ourselves looking back at our poster on the wall. It is beginning to bloom with colored hearts carrying the names of those we offer to God as we continue our Lenten journey.

An Overview of Living the Beatitudes

- Eight beatitudes are offered within the six weeks of Lent. Each beatitude is introduced with a photograph and a companion reading. At the beginning of each week, the beatitude reflection is read and a photograph or picture illustrating it is posted on the backdrop.

- A version of each week's beatitude is read every day.

- "The Word to Ponder" gives an example of someone living the beatitude and offers suggestions about how others might live the beatitude today.

- "Bringing People Into the Heart of God" offers time to share together and pray for others. You will find yourselves praying for friends and loved ones, difficult people in your life, tragedies that appear in the news and many other people and events. Each day write the names of those for whom you want to pray on a cutout and put the cutout on a backdrop.

- Close with the Lord's Prayer. You may also want to sing together.

Getting Ready to Pray With Living the Beatitudes

Use some, all or none of these suggestions to create your prayer. Let this book support your imaginative prayer style.

Choose a space for gathering each day to share together and to pray. It could be the dining room table, the family room or the living room. Decorate the space with a candle, a sacred image, flowers, whatever speaks to you of God. *Remember to use caution with candles, especially if young children are present!*

In a basket or other container, gather tape, scissors, pens and cutout shapes. We have included patterns on page 104; trace them if

John B.

you wish and transfer them to colored construction paper. Cut them out before the prayer time.

Hang a backdrop in your gathering space to hold the cutouts: a large piece of colored cardboard, a large poster that is simple and appropriate to the Lenten season, a large cloth or sheet. The backdrop will become heavier as you affix the cutouts, so anchor it well. As you move through Lent to Easter, the backdrop blossoms with color!

Each week, choose a photograph from family albums, newspapers or magazines to depict the beatitude of the week. Place the photo on the backdrop; during the week arrange the cutouts around the photo.

Involve as many people as possible in preparing the space, cutting out the shapes, lighting the candle, reading, sharing, praying, choosing photos and selecting songs. Doing even these simple tasks with great love makes the Beatitudes visible in our lives.

Blessed are the poor in spirit,
  for theirs is the kingdom of heaven.

Blessed are those who mourn,
  for they will be comforted.

Blessed are the meek,
  for they will inherit the earth.

Blessed are those who hunger and thirst
    for righteousness,
  for they will be filled.

Blessed are the merciful,
  for they will receive mercy.

Blessed are the pure in heart,
  for they will see God.

Blessed are the peacemakers,
  for they will be called children of God.

Blessed are those who are persecuted
    for righteousness' sake,
  for theirs is the kingdom of heaven.

—Matthew 5:3-10

The Hunger for Righteousness

Henri, Gail, Francis, Sue

*Blessed are those who hunger
and thirst for righteousness,
for they will be filled.*

The business world is a hungry world. Within its competitive walls, people work hard and live on adrenaline. Success is held out as an incentive. Work hard enough and you will find wealth, power, respect. Make it big enough and your hunger will be satisfied. Reach the top and you can relax and stop struggling.

Gail knew this world intimately. She worked hard to become a leader in her field. She was one of the hungry ones. But she found that success didn't satisfy her hunger in the long run. She couldn't relax and take it easy. In order to keep her place on the ladder, she had to stay competitive, stay productive, stay hungry.

Looking down, Gail could see that she was living in a world of famine. She was being starved so that her hunger would be fueled, not filled. Money and power did not buy freedom from want. They kept her in a cycle of increasing hunger that made her work harder, longer, faster.

When Gail entered the L'Arche community she made a choice to break that cycle. She recognized that her deepest hunger was for peace, for love, for home. While community can be hard work, it offered Gail a better chance to satisfy her deepest hunger.

Gail chose to be confirmed during our community worship service at Easter. It was a symbol of her commitment to nourish her body and spirit in community. In a world of famine and hunger Gail stood up to announce the good news of abundant love and hope. She is discovering that her deepest hunger can be satisfied in relationships of love and forgiveness.

Ash Wednesday

*Gather in a circle and light a candle. Begin with the
following readings.*

The Beatitude

Blessed are you when you yearn for what is right and
good, for you will be satisfied.

The Word to Ponder

The argument was not a friendly one. It was happening
at dinner when ten of us were gathered around the
table. I had challenged Paul to shower before coming
to the table. He worked in the barn; I found the smell
of the barn unpleasant and believed others did, too.
Paul responded that this was his house and he could
decide for himself when he would shower. Paul and I
each thought we were defending what was right, but
our words were wounding each other and creating
tension at the table.

After supper I was still fuming from the exchange.
Frank, who had been present at the table, pulled me
aside and said, "So, you and Paul are not doing very
well!" "Never mind, Frank," I replied. "Paul and I have
to sort that out!" Frank thought for a moment, looked
me in the eye and very gently said, "You know, if you
want to help Paul, you have to love him."

Jesus invites us to be gentle when there is a question
between us about who is right and who is wrong. With
great love for us, Jesus tells us to love our enemies.
For each of us this is a powerful invitation to look at
one another with new eyes and to speak to each other
with love and with care.

Bringing People Into the Heart of God

*Write names and intentions on the cutout. Read them
aloud and ask God's blessing on those named and all
present. Attach the cutout to the backdrop, near the
photograph for the week. End with the Lord's Prayer and a
song.*

Thursday After Ash Wednesday

Gather in a circle and light a candle. Begin with the following readings.

The Beatitude

You are blessed if you desire the good and the true. You will find it, and you will be filled with it.

The Word to Ponder

Roy, now eighty years of age, spent fifty years in a mental hospital before coming to L'Arche. He is down-to-earth, true to the core of his being, a humble man in the best sense of the word. He has a great gift for greeting. His instinctive gesture when meeting someone is to extend his hand, announce the person's name and engage in conversation. Roy is eager to welcome and to trust, even though he is often misunderstood and wounded in his relationships.

Jesus says that when we welcome one another, we welcome him. Today let us pray for the courage to risk welcoming one another with sacred acceptance and care.

Bringing People Into the Heart of God

Write names and intentions on the cutout. Read them aloud and ask God's blessing on those named and all present. Attach the cutout to the backdrop, near the photograph for the week. End with the Lord's Prayer and a song.

Friday After Ash Wednesday

Gather in a circle and light a candle. Begin with the following readings.

The Beatitude

You are happy if you live from your thirst for goodness and righteousness, for you shall be filled with grace.

The Word to Ponder

Thelis is deeply sensitive; she knows quickly whether people take her seriously or not, and she suffers when they do not. She knows about anger, too. Sometimes it surges up, making her feel bossy and controlling. But Thelis never closes her door.

With deep sincerity Thelis says, "I like to welcome people to my house and to cook a meal for them. I like to visit the sick, to bake for people in need, to pray for poor people who have nothing to eat and to be a friend to someone who needs me. All these things make me feel good."

God's word invites us to be true to our hearts and steadfast. Do not be disturbed in times of difficulty. You will be tested by these times, like gold that is tested in fire, and like the gold, your value will be revealed. Today try to live from your desire to be a person of peace.

Bringing People Into the Heart of God

Write names and intentions on the cutout. Read them aloud and ask God's blessing on those named and all present. Attach the cutout to the backdrop, near the photograph for the week. End with the Lord's Prayer and a song.

Saturday After Ash Wednesday

Gather in a circle and light a candle. Begin with the following readings.

The Beatitude

When you hope for what is good and right, for what is true and of God, you are recognized and blessed by the God who loves you.

The Word to Ponder

Michael A. loves our pastor, Henri. When Henri is absent, Michael will say, "I miss Henri. I miss him right here, in my heart!" When Henri returns, Michael tells him, "You were away. It hurt me, in my heart!" Michael knows that we need each other to live. Our love for one another helps us. Without it we experience too much loneliness, weakness and sadness.

Jesus tells us that before we gather to pray we need to make sure that our relationships with one another are healthy and that we tell each other of our love.

Bringing People Into the Heart of God

Write names and intentions on the cutout. Read them aloud and ask God's blessing on those named and all present. Attach the cutout to the backdrop, near the photograph for the week. End with the Lord's Prayer and a song.

Blessed Are Those Who Mourn

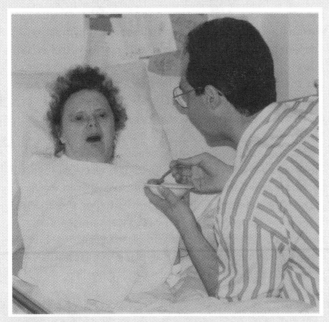

Helen, Tony

Blessed are those who mourn, for they will be comforted.

Helen H. is dying of Alzheimer's disease. Each day robs her of memories and skills and separates her from the funny and joyful person she was before. Helen can no longer embarrass us with birthday cards that read "In deepest sympathy." She can't scandalize the local store clerks with her tall tales of how she'd been kidnapped. She'll never again put the pastor in his place by snoring in the front pew when he gets long-winded. Even while her spirit is very much alive, her body and mind are letting go, and we mourn her passing.

But something profoundly beautiful is happening as Helen grows weaker. She is building a circle of love around herself that keeps her joy alive. When we gather with Helen we find ourselves telling the stories she can no longer speak. Our laughter and tears witness to her life and draw us closer together. Her bedside has become a meeting place of past and present, and people find there tender healing, forgiveness and hope.

This is not an easy process. There are days when Helen is racked by seizures or lost in her confusion. In these moments her eyes are full of fear, and she begs us to hold her hand and stay close. Perhaps because she has loved us so well, we are able to give her the support she needs to continue the difficult journey of letting go. And Helen gives us the gift of her spirit so that we can continue the difficult journey of living.

Encircled with the love of her family and community, Helen died on November 8, 1994. May the angels rejoice with her.

Sunday of the First Week of Lent

Gather in a circle and light a candle. Begin with the following readings.

The Beatitude

Blessed are you if you are in mourning, for you will be comforted.

The Word to Ponder

Even though we knew that Maurice was dying, his death made us very sad. He was a light in our midst and a joy to know. We miss him, so we talk about him to one another, and we keep his photo in our chapel space. We remember how each year he would invite us to his "Happy Birthday Party." When we sing, we speak of him and how he would begin the hymn *Amazing Grace* every chance he could find. We still imitate him at the dinner table by saying "Tastes goooood" the way he said it.

Blessed comes from the Latin word *benediction*, which means to say (*dicere*) good things (*bene*) about someone. We've blessed Maurice so much before and since his death. Our love for and our blessing of him is but a small sign of the love and blessing that comes to each one of us from the One who loves us with a never-ending love.

When you gather in my name, Jesus says, I am in your midst. We can grieve together, hold onto each other, talk about our sorrow and know that God is with us, saying good words to help us live some of the pain of our losses.

Bringing People Into the Heart of God

Write names and intentions on the cutout. Read them aloud and ask God's blessing on those named and all present. Attach the cutout to the backdrop, near the photograph for the week. End with the Lord's Prayer and a song.

Monday of the First Week of Lent

Gather in a circle and light a candle. Begin with the following readings.

The Beatitude

Blessed are those who mourn, for they will be comforted.

The Word to Ponder

Upset because of something someone said to her, Loretta left the house without telling anyone. We looked in all the familiar places, but she was gone. The police finally found her several hours later. She clearly did not want to communicate on her return, so she went and sat alone in the TV room, her arms folded over her chest and her eyes closed. She did not want any supper, but she did stay with the group in the TV room during the evening. At bedtime she invited one of the assistants to pray with her. As soon as the assistant sat down on the edge of her bed, Loretta burst into tears and wept into her hands. Later, when she looked up, she could only say, "It hurts. It hurts too much in my heart."

Loretta's cry finds an echo in each of us. There are times when each of us also says, "It hurts. It hurts too much in my heart." Jesus, just after the Last Supper, in the garden of Gethsemane, said something similar. He was talking to his Father, saying, "Please take away this pain because it is too much for me." We know that Jesus is the Chosen One, the Beloved of the Father. So is Loretta chosen. So are you and I. Jesus came to break any ties between pain and punishment. Our God is close to the broken-hearted—to you and to me.

Bringing People Into the Heart of God

Write names and intentions on the cutout. Read them aloud and ask God's blessing on those named and all present. Attach the cutout to the backdrop, near the photograph for the week. End with the Lord's Prayer and a song.

Tuesday of the First Week of Lent

Gather in a circle and light a candle. Begin with the following readings.

God is close to the brokenhearted.

The Spirit Movers, a dance ensemble of community members, have touched people from the moment they began dancing. Gracefully and artfully, children and adults, men and women, those in wheelchairs and those on their toes perform the dance. They dance in our churches, and they dance when we give public talks.

Marcie is the inspiration behind the Spirit Movers. She is a true artist, a dancer to the core, and whenever she introduces the group, her eyes fill with tears. The Spirit Movers move her spirit.

When we are connected to the deepest aspirations of our hearts, we sometimes find ourselves in tears. The feeling isn't sadness, but there is an anguish that rises up and is beyond our control. We may feel embarrassed to have others see us in tears. But Jesus teaches us that tears are sacred. Our weeping is often a priceless reminder of the deep sensitivity of our hearts, hearts that yearn with others to be part of the dance of life.

Write names and intentions on the cutout. Read them aloud and ask God's blessing on those named and all present. Attach the cutout to the backdrop, near the photograph for the week. End with the Lord's Prayer and a song.

Wednesday of the First Week of Lent

Gather in a circle and light a candle. Begin with the
following readings.

The Beatitude

When you are sad, God is close to you.

The Word to Ponder

Sue told about the time she was falling apart:
"I needed to take some time away from being
responsible, but I didn't want to leave the community,
so I asked to live in the home where the core
members were more independent and did not have
live-in assistants.

"Peter R., David G., Thelis, Annie and Peggy listened
as I told them that I was not very strong inside and that
I needed a safe place to stay while I tried to see what
was happening to me. I told them that sometimes I
couldn't stop crying, and I did not want that to frighten
them.

"With open arms they welcomed me. At the Sunday
night house meeting Peggy said, 'We take turns to do
the shopping, but you do not have to have a turn
unless you want one. If you want anything, just put it
on the list and we will get it for you.' 'Yes,' said Thelis,
'and we take turns doing the cooking, but you don't
have to cook unless you want to.' I was crying just
listening to her!

"Annie gave me space in her closet and emptied the
top drawer of her dresser to accommodate some of
my things. Peter usually bought me some candy on his
way home from work each night. David consistently
said, 'I'm so glad you're living with us!' I felt so limited
in my ability to respond to the love that they
showered upon me, but they helped to heal my tired
and broken heart."

Within each one of us are unshed tears. Few times
and places seem safe enough for us to "break down"
and experience the healing power of our tears.
Perhaps we need to ensure that we all have someplace
where we have the safety to grieve. God calls us

"blessed" when we mourn. We may not understand how it happens, but God is near, loving us and yearning to help us to believe how deeply we are cherished in God's heart.

Bringing People Into the Heart of God

Write names and intentions on the cutout. Read them aloud and ask God's blessing on those named and all present. Attach the cutout to the backdrop, near the photograph for the week. End with the Lord's Prayer and a song.

Thursday of the First Week of Lent

Gather in a circle and light a candle. Begin with the following readings.

The Beatitude

Blessed are you when your heart is heavy, for God is compassionate and caring.

The Word to Ponder

After forty-two years, Carol was moving from the state hospital into her first home. As people moved her belongings and helped arrange her room, she noticed they were putting a large mirror on the wall. "Stop," she said. "Don't put that mirror in my room!" "Why not?" someone asked. "Because I will never look into it!" replied Carol. "But why would you never look into the mirror?" asked the helper. "Because I hate myself so much," said Carol. "Well," answered the helper, "I think we will put it here anyway. Someday, you may want to look at yourself."

Carol, who told this story herself, went on to say, "One day, after about two years, I did decide to look in the mirror. I looked, and then I said to myself, 'You know, you aren't so bad after all!'"

A dark voice within tells me I am worthless and without friends. Hearing the voice, my heart is heavy and sad. I feel disgusted and uncomfortable. Jesus, knowing this, invites us to love one another and to become mirrors of truth for each other. I am a mirror for you. If I look at you with distaste, you will begin to hear that dark voice rising up to haunt you and make you feel miserable. You are a mirror for me. When you look at me with respect and love, I feel that I am beautiful.

Bringing People Into the Heart of God

Write names and intentions on the cutout. Read them aloud and ask God's blessing on those named and all present. Attach the cutout to the backdrop, near the photograph for the week. End with the Lord's Prayer and a song.

Friday of the First Week of Lent

Gather in a circle and light a candle. Begin with the following readings.

The Beatitude

Do you know that your tears are sacred to God, that your tears reveal a deeply sensitive heart?

The Word to Ponder

By the time she was twenty-six Joanne had lived in twenty-six foster homes, yet she had never forgotten her mother. She pleaded with her family to be able to go home for Christmas and received a reluctant "OK." She told us, "I want to buy my mother a really nice present. And I will buy something special for each of my sisters and for my brother." Knowing how sensitive she was and how much this visit meant to her, we called ahead to say that Joanne was bringing gifts.

When we arrived at her home around four in the afternoon on Christmas day, the family was watching TV and told us we could make a cup of tea for ourselves in the kitchen where Joanne's grandmother was sitting, alone. Later, when the family joined us, Joanne presented her beautifully wrapped presents. People were grateful. Each one then had a gift for Joanne, but each of the seven gifts was a bottle of perfume. Joanne graciously thanked those who had remembered her with a gift. Then, because they had had their main meal at noon, they invited us to make ourselves a turkey sandwich for supper. Joanne cried on the way home and asked, "Why am I retarded?" It hurts to feel unwanted. Rejection taps into that very deep fear that we're not lovable.

Jesus was betrayed with a kiss, a sign of love, and was captured and put to death, although he had done nothing wrong. Even in his agony, though, Jesus was the blessed Son of God. So too, in her agony is Joanne a blessed daughter of God. You and I are beloved daughters and sons. Our suffering is not a punishment; it is a mystery. And God is close to the brokenhearted.

25

Bringing People Into the Heart of God

Write names and intentions on the cutout. Read them aloud and ask God's blessing on those named and all present. Attach the cutout to the backdrop, near the photograph for the week. End with the Lord's Prayer and a song.

Saturday of the First Week of Lent

Gather in a circle and light a candle. Begin with the following readings.

The Beatitude

Blessed are those who mourn, for they will be comforted.

The Word to Ponder

Jeanne had recently buried her mother. Feeling unwell, she decided to stay in bed for the day. Her son, Michael A., home from Daybreak for the weekend, sat with her on the side of her bed, simply holding her hand. She was sad, and Michael was a comfort to her.

Rex, her husband, came into the room, and Michael, staring at a short gold vase of roses, said in a halting and stuttering way, "Put some Coke into that." Rex explained that the vase was for flowers only. Mike insisted, "Put some Coke into the vase." When he realized that it wasn't worth an argument, Rex filled the vase with Coke.

Michael took the vase and disappeared into the living room for quite some time. When he reappeared, he invited his parents to follow him to the living room. He had put three chairs around the coffee table. On the table was a slice of bread on a plate and the vase filled with Coke.

When they were seated, Michael said, "Now we will pray for Grandma." He broke the bread and passed some to each one to eat. Then he took the vase, raised it high and passed it to each one to drink.

Michael prayed, "Now God, I want you to look after my grandma." After a long period of quiet, Michael looked up and said to his parents, "Now we have prayed for Grandma, and God will take care of her. But we also have to think of Grandpa, because he is alone. Can we go to see him this afternoon?"

Michael is not scandalized by another's tears. Like God, he wants to offer comfort. Michael's heart is connected with his mother's heart, just as God's heart is connected to each of ours. We are God's beloved

27

daughters and sons. Our pain draws forth the compassion of the God of love.

Bringing People Into the Heart of God

Write names and intentions on the cutout. Read them aloud and ask God's blessing on those named and all present. Attach the cutout to the backdrop, near the photograph for the week. End with the Lord's Prayer and a song.

The Meek Will Inherit the Earth

Monica Anne, Carrie

Blessed are the meek,
for they will inherit the earth.

There's not enough—not enough money, not enough land, not enough love. All the violence of our age seems to confirm this fact. If you want something you have to fight for it. There is no place for weakness in a world that takes survival of the strongest as gospel.

But how do we explain the story of Monica Anne? She was just a newborn baby when we learned that she had a heart problem and required immediate surgery. How is it she had the power to make us forget ourselves and support her family and worry about her well-being? Why was our joy at her recovery greater than anything we could feel for ourselves?

It's easy to forget these anxious moments and these questions now as we watch Monica Anne sit with her mother and play with her sister. But we must not forget them because they hold the key to a secret we must uncover.

In her illness Monica Anne bestowed a blessing on every member of our community. She broke through our barriers and brought us together. She made us stronger as a community by making us open up to welcome her fragility and her littleness.

In the face of the overwhelming struggles of our world, Monica Anne is a sign of blessing. She helps us grasp the gift hidden in weakness. Perhaps only the strong can survive in a hostile and fearful world. But only those who welcome littleness can transform that world of fear into a land of abundant joy. Monica Anne and the littlest ones are here to bless us as we make the journey from fear to joy.

Sunday of the Second Week of Lent

*Gather in a circle and light a candle. Begin with the
following readings.*

The Beatitude

Blessed are the meek, for they will inherit the earth.

The Word to Ponder

When Janice was a child, she lost her favorite brother
in a tragic drowning. It was at this time that she ceased
speaking and relating to people. As a mature woman,
she continues more or less to "stand alone,"
pretending she does not understand or is not
interested in what goes on around her. Jan only
responds when we insist and she pushes us away, or
when we cajole and she bursts out laughing, or when
the word of God is being announced and she surprises
us by her openness!

Jan was part of a small group accompanying our
pastor, Henri, who was speaking to a large group of
social workers. Although she had said yes to going, Jan
related little with those who spoke with her, and she
sat apart from the rest of the group. We wondered
about inviting her to participate in the mime of the
Last Supper, but once again she said yes to playing the
part of one of the disciples.

Jan put herself totally into the scene, focusing on
"Jesus" and drinking in the things he was saying, even
putting her head down on the table in sadness when he
announced that he was "going away." At this point
"Jesus" approached her and touched her on the
shoulder, at which point she turned, looked into his
eyes, opened her arms and embraced him. Her eyes
never left him as he gently washed her feet, and she
simply rested in peace as he moved to wash the feet of
the next person.

If we can open ourselves to the beauty and the
depth of meaning in the washing of the feet, Jesus' love
will break open our closed hearts. This mysterious
gesture—God kneeling and washing his apostles' feet,
then inviting them to do likewise—is but a sign of the

overflowing heart of the Divine! Let us put ourselves there and receive the outpouring of God's mercy and love. Through this experience, may we "know" how to wash one another!

Bringing People Into the Heart of God

Write names and intentions on the cutout. Read them aloud and ask God's blessing on those named and all present. Attach the cutout to the backdrop, near the photograph for the week. End with the Lord's Prayer and a song.

Monday of the Second Week of Lent

Gather in a circle and light a candle. Begin with the following readings.

The Beatitude

When you try to follow in the footsteps of Jesus, you will be pleasing in the eyes of God.

The Word to Ponder

Bill was unhappy in his job at the hospital, and we were trying to help him to stick with it, but he was not impressed. Each morning he greeted us with the words, "I don't want to go to work! I hate that job. The people don't like me. They make me do all the hard jobs. I hate always having to empty the garbage. Please don't make me go to work."

When we realized that all Bill said was true, we told him that it would be good to quit, but not until his vacation began in one week's time. That final week was a huge effort. We tried to reassure Bill that he could do it and that he could then leave with dignity on Friday.

Friday morning we gave him a pep talk. "One more day!" we said. "You can do it, Bill! In fact you can have a good day! Just decide that today will be a really good day. Try not to let their remarks and their laughter get to you. Just know that tomorrow you will be on vacation! So remember that you can decide what kind of a day you'll have. Will it be a good day?"

Bill reluctantly said, "OK, I'll try, but I hate it anyway."

At noon the phone rang. Bill asked for the head of the house and said, "I'm having a really good day, but could you come and get me? I got fired!"

God's Spirit speaks from within us in a still, small voice, "You are my beloved, my cherished one. On you my favor rests." Connected to that voice, we receive power to live a good day even when we experience disillusionment in our work or in our lives.

Bringing People Into the Heart of God

Write names and intentions on the cutout. Read them aloud and ask God's blessing on those named and all present. Attach the cutout to the backdrop, near the photograph for the week. End with the Lord's Prayer and a song.

Tuesday of the Second Week of Lent

Gather in a circle and light a candle. Begin with the following readings.

The Beatitude

Happy are you when you stay connected with the voice of love that calls you from within.

The Word to Ponder

Janet stopped Henri as he came into the chapel area to celebrate the Eucharist. "I want you to give me a blessing," she said. Without thinking much about it, Henri responded, "Janet, God bless you in the name of the Father, the Son and the Holy Spirit." "Oh no!" said Janet, "That is not good enough. I want a real blessing." Henri, taken aback, apologized and asked Janet to wait until the end of the eucharistic celebration.

When Mass was over, Henri said to the group, "Before this celebration, Janet asked me for a blessing. I was in a hurry then, but now I am ready. So, Janet could you come forward?" Henri held out his arms, and Janet walked right up to him so that her head was close to his chest. He gently laid his hands on her head and said, "Janet, God has made you into such a beautiful woman, and I believe that God loves you very dearly. God wants you to know that you are a wonderful person, and God wants you to continue to be a loving person in your family and in the community and beyond. Go now, and remember that you are loved and that you have the gift of love to give to others."

Janet turned to sit down and almost at once Mary Anne said, "What about me? I want a blessing too!" When she turned to go, Greg was there, followed by Patsy, Karen, Julie, Kim, John and many others.

In our community we often encircle someone who is leaving to preach a retreat or to help in another community. We put our hands on the person, saying at the same time a word of encouragement, "God is a loving God. You are loved by God. Go now, knowing

that God's Spirit accompanies you at every moment of your life."

Before bringing others into the heart of God, let those who desire a blessing ask for it: a parent of a child, a spouse of a spouse, a child of a parent, a sister of a brother, a friend of a friend.

Bringing People Into the Heart of God

Write names and intentions on the cutout. Read them aloud and ask God's blessing on those named and all present. Attach the cutout to the backdrop, near the photograph for the week. End with the Lord's Prayer and a song.

Wednesday of the Second Week of Lent

Gather in a circle and light a candle. Begin with the following readings.

The Beatitude

As you live with your weakness and vulnerability, you are cherished in God's sight.

The Word to Ponder

Hsi Fu is a man who waits. Visually impaired, he waits to be bathed and dressed in the morning, then he waits till his breakfast is ready and there is someone free to feed him. He waits for help to be "walked" to his wheelchair and taken to school each day, and then he waits for someone to help him with his exercises and other activities. He has to wait to be fed his lunch and then he rests until it is time to be taken back to class for the afternoon. After school, when he is at home again, Hsi Fu waits for dinner to be ready and for the one who will help him get the food on the fork and into his mouth. In the evening he waits to be taken swimming or shopping, or he sits in a chair or on the floor, listening and smiling. He loves a joke, a pillow fight or a wrestle, and then we hear his laughter! He often falls asleep while waiting for bedtime. Having learned so well how to wait, Hsi Fu radiates a spirit of peace and contentment. For all that he receives, he returns joy!

We often spend our time trying to figure out why we are suffering and who is to blame for the brokenness of our hearts or our lives. Hsi Fu is a wonderful teacher. He has come to terms with his life as it is, and he wastes no time, though he has lots of it, in bitterness and self-rejection. Perhaps today we can step over some of our pain to welcome our lives as they are, and thus become people of acceptance and peace.

Jesus invites us to come to him with our burdens, angers and fears. He is prepared to work wonders for us in helping us to see the larger picture. Our life, *as it is*, is special.

Bringing People Into the Heart of God

Write names and intentions on the cutout. Read them aloud and ask God's blessing on those named and all present. Attach the cutout to the backdrop, near the photograph for the week. End with the Lord's Prayer and a song.

Thursday of the Second Week of Lent

Gather in a circle and light a candle. Begin with the following readings.

The Beatitude

How happy are you when you find strength in God to live from the truth of your life.

The Word to Ponder

Peter P.'s anxiety causes him to ask the same questions over and over again: "Am I going to go to church on Sunday? St. John's? Will you drive me to church on Sunday? Is Julie going to be at church? Going to church on Sunday?" By about 3 P.M. on Saturdays, the people in the home have had it with Peter! We have answered each question at least forty times; we have stopped Peter to make certain he heard the answers; we have teased him and cajoled him; we have told him, "Cut it! Not a good question!" His anxiety drives him. Our patience wears thin.

One day, in jest, I raised my hand as if to strike him and said, "Peter, my elbow has a spring attached to it and every time the word *church* is said, the spring goes off. You better watch out in case you get hit!" I tapped him on the cheek. He laughed and cried out, "Don't hit me, Sue!"

I responded by saying, "Oh Peter, that one was gentle. That was a love tap compared to what is coming if you don't think of something else to say!"

Peter looked serious for a moment, then with a beautiful smile he said, "Give me another love tap, Sue."

Jesus did not come to take our vulnerability away. He teaches us how to live together as vulnerable people. We need to discover how we find the grace and the strengh to ask for and give a love tap to one another, especially when we feel anxious or frustrated.

Bringing People Into the Heart of God

Write names and intentions on the cutout. Read them aloud and ask God's blessing on those named and all present. Attach the cutout to the backdrop, near the photograph for the week. End with the Lord's Prayer and a song.

Friday of the Second Week of Lent

Gather in a circle and light a candle. Begin with the following readings.

The Beatitude

Blessed are you when you welcome the truth of your life as a gift and not as a problem.

The Word to Ponder

Patsy has very short arms and has difficulty with zippers. She moves slowly, but because she suffers from the cold she never approaches the door until she is fully dressed, even though it seems to take ages. She huffs and puffs while she struggles again and again to capture the ends of the coat and connect the zipper.

After a brunch with the Egan family, Patsy was preparing for departure in her customary fashion. Patrick, age five, noticed her stuggle and asked, "Patsy, can I give you a hand with your zipper?" When Patsy said yes, Patrick knelt down in front of her, gently took her coat in his small hands and zipped it to the top. His eyes moved up to meet Patsy's. She was smiling a broad smile as she took his head into her hands, kissed him on the top of it, and said with great meaning, "Thank you."

The "zippers" of our lives can be cause for despair or an opportunity for a meaningful encounter! Why do we hide the fact that sometimes we are slow to make connections? Why do we huff and puff about our problems instead of asking for help and allowing ourselves the privilege of thanking one another? This is the call of the gospel.

Bringing People Into the Heart of God

Write names and intentions on the cutout. Read them aloud and ask God's blessing on those named and all present. Attach the cutout to the backdrop, near the photograph for the week. End with the Lord's Prayer and a song.

Saturday of the Second Week of Lent

Gather in a circle and light a candle. Begin with the following readings.

The Beatitude

Blessed are you when you welcome the truth of your life as a gift and not as a problem.

The Word to Ponder

"The new person in the home was speaking out of a certain frustration, but when I heard her telling Mary Anne that she must stop talking about her birthday, I reacted strongly," recounted Mary, one of the longtime assistants. "Mary Anne taught me to appreciate my birthday!" Mary said, and she went on to tell the story.

"Mary Anne loves birthdays and not just her own. Although she doesn't remember some of the things that would be helpful for her, her awareness of birthdays is colossal! First thing in the morning she announces who is having a birthday. Long gone assistants, people who are away, those who live in other homes, are all remembered and each is prayed for at the evening quiet time. Mary Anne talks about the person and hopes that she will be invited to the party.

"Mary Anne begins talking about and planning her own December birthday in October. I, on the other hand, have always been embarrassed around my birthday, feeling ambivalent and not telling others about my special day. Then I feel upset because no one remembered me. Most of us have trouble sharing Mary Anne's excitement and, like the new person in the home, we try to put a cap on the birthday conversations. But Mary Anne is not to be shut down. She is excited because it is her special day, because she will have her favorite meal, because her friends will come and because her life will be celebrated. Mary Anne is delighted to be alive and to be celebrated!

"Entering into her excitement instead of trying to close her off forced me to think about my ambivalence

about my own birthday. I love her enthusiasm and pure joy and because of her I'm definitely changing. I'm beginning to accept more, to wonder more, and to celebrate more the precious jewel that is my life."

May each of us profit by Mary Anne's teaching!

Bringing People Into the Heart of God

Write names and intentions on the cutout. Read them aloud and ask God's blessing on those named and all present. Attach the cutout to the backdrop, near the photograph for the week. End with the Lord's Prayer and a song.

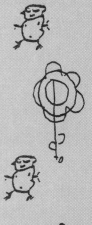

The Peacemakers Are the Children of God

Tracy, Doug

Blessed are the peacemakers, for they will be called children of God.

The word *peacemakers* calls to mind images of U.N. soldiers in burned-out villages in Bosnia, Somalia and Rwanda. They need blue helmets, guns and armored cars. They often must use force to restore a peace that seldom lasts.

But this is not the only way to be a peacemaker. Other ways lead to a peace that lasts. Special people in our lives show us how to make lasting peace in our hearts, our homes, our communities.

Doug is one of these people. As a Mennonite he sees peacemaking as a way of life and a part of every relationship. He is gentle and soft-spoken, yet passionate in his commitment to the struggle for peace and justice. In our community Doug is faithful to those who "disturb the peace" because they cannot control their anger and violence. Day by day Doug is there— standing on the other side of anger, ready to forgive and try again.

Tracy is another person who lives peacemaking at the center of her life. When she calls her friends to help her with her bath or move her out of her wheelchair or sit with her on the mat, she asks them to touch her with gentleness and respect. She asks them to make peace within themselves so that they can reach out to her with peacefulness.

During our community prayer services Doug and Tracy often sit together. Doug enfolds Tracy with his gentle embrace, and she encircles him with her joyful smile. The embrace lasts but a moment, but it is a sign that reminds us all that peacemaking is personal work and that lasting peace finds its seeds in such simple gestures.

Sunday of the Third Week of Lent

Gather in a circle and light a candle. Begin with the following readings.

The Beatitude

Blessed are the peacemakers, for they will be called the children of God.

The Word to Ponder

Julie loves her flower garden, but it's difficult to keep the flowers from those who like to pick them! One summer day she went out to enjoy her last surviving gladiolus, only to find that it was gone! Spotting Trevor not far away, she immediately asked, "Trevor, did you take my last glad?" Trevor smiled innocently and replied, "No, I didn't take it." Then he pulled the flower from his back pocket and with great warmth said, "Here, Julie, I picked this for you this morning!"

Very often we misconstrue a gesture that another uses to express affection. When Jesus tried to wash Peter's feet at the Last Supper, Peter was outraged and refused. Jesus quietly asks him to trust that what he is doing will later be understood as something very meaningful, to trust that what looks ridiculous is, in fact, a gesture of deep tenderness and love.

Parents might want to give a bit more space before correcting their children. Children and others of us might want to be more open to gestures that seem overly corrective or even oppressive. By trusting one another over and over again, even after trust has been broken, we build peace between us.

Bringing People Into the Heart of God

Write names and intentions on the cutout. Read them aloud and ask God's blessing on those named and all present. Attach the cutout to the backdrop, near the photograph for the week. End with the Lord's Prayer and a song.

Monday of the Third Week of Lent

Gather in a circle and light a candle. Begin with the following readings.

The Beatitude

If you forgive each other, you will be waging peace instead of war, and you will own the earth.

The Word to Ponder

Mel has lived in the house for many years. Patrick B. arrived only a year ago, and the two are getting to know each other, but slowly. They are very different men, so it takes time. When Mel was celebrating his birthday with all his friends on a Sunday afternoon, Patrick stayed upstairs in his room, refusing all invitations to come down and be with his housemate on his special day.

Then something beautiful happened. After supper, Patrick quietly asked Mel if he could treat him to an ice cream. Mel accepted and off they went. An hour later they came back, talking together.

Jesus would tell us that Patrick's choice to invite Mel and Mel's choice to accept embody his teachings about love. Today, in our many relationships, we can follow their good example.

Bringing People Into the Heart of God

Write names and intentions on the cutout. Read them aloud and ask God's blessing on those named and all present. Attach the cutout to the backdrop, near the photograph for the week. End with the Lord's Prayer and a song.

Tuesday of the Third Week of Lent

Gather in a circle and light a candle. Begin with the following readings.

The Beatitude

Be people who bring peace, and walk freely upon the earth.

The Word to Ponder

Carol is often the source of joy in her home. She does not speak, but she appears to understand everything that happens around her. One day, she came to the dinner table and suddenly burst into tears. Others at the table waited silently, not knowing exactly how to respond. Maurice, a man of deep compassion, turned to Julie and said, "Is Carol crying because her father is dead or because her mother is dead?" Julie answered, "Mo, I really don't know." Mo waited another minute before taking hold of the situation. He began to pray, "Dear Lord, please help Carol. She is probably sad because her father is dead. Please look after Carol's father." Carol looked up, found Maurice with her eyes, got up, walked over and from behind gave Maurice a hug. Then she returned to her place, ready for dinner.

Compassion is the gift of the peace-builder. Those who wage peace focus energy and love toward building a bridge between themselves and others who are suffering or angry or isolated. Jesus invites us, "Do unto others as you would want them to do to you."

Bringing People Into the Heart of God

Write names and intentions on the cutout. Read them aloud and ask God's blessing on those named and all present. Attach the cutout to the backdrop, near the photograph for the week. End with the Lord's Prayer and a song.

Wednesday of the Third Week of Lent

Gather in a circle and light a candle. Begin with the following readings.

The Beatitude

The heart of the peacemaker is like the heart of God, owning the earth as an inheritance.

The Word to Ponder

Through a break in communication, the other members of the household did not feel empowered by or even part of the decision to welcome Gordon F. into the home. They were rightly hurt and angry, but Gordon was coming anyway.

Gordon arrived with his long history of institutional living and with all his "different" behaviors, such as chewing his shirt and yelling some of his responses. The situation was tense...for about a week. By that time, Gordon was finding his way into each person's heart, and people were opening up to his presence. Within a month he had taken his rightful place. Before long, people of the household were asking how they had ever lived without him. With time, some of the behaviors disappeared, returning only when Gordon felt insecure in his home.

Gordon needs a lot of assistance, but he responds to those who help him with huge smiles and hugs. By his very person he challenges us to be united and to work together, because when our relationships are fragmented and broken, Gordon feels the vibes and cannot cope. Secure or not, Gord is a source of unity in our midst.

Saint Paul speaks about this mystery to the Corinthians when he asks them to consider their call. He tells them and us that not many are wise and not many powerful, but our God chooses what is foolish in the world to shame the wise and chooses what is weak in the world to shame the strong. He suggests that God hides within and behind the weakest of this world. May we have new eyes to recognize God's presence in our midst.

Write names and intentions on the cutout. Read them aloud and ask God's blessing on those named and all present. Attach the cutout to the backdrop, near the photograph for the week. End with the Lord's Prayer and a song.

Thursday of the Third Week of Lent

Gather in a circle and light a candle. Begin with the following readings.

The Beatitude

Blessed are those who make peace. They will be enriched.

The Word to Ponder

The theme of our day of reflection together had been the story of the Prodigal Son. To close the day we shared a meal and enacted the gospel story. Greg and Karen played the parents, while Kathy and her four-year-old son, Timmy, played the role of the younger son. Gord H. was the elder son.

Toward the end of our meal, Kathy and Timmy, role-playing the story, stood up and announced that they wanted their inheritance because they were going to New York to live it up. They said many hurtful things about the "family"—that it was square, boring, narrow and stupid and that they couldn't wait to get free from such a stifling environment. Greg, as father, quietly counted out some money and gave it to them, after which they left the table.

The rest of us, wondering together what had taken possession of our "siblings" who had left, began to clean up after the meal. When the dishes were done, we went downstairs to the chapel. Kathy and Tim, having spent the inheritance, were huddled into a corner, bedraggled and dirty. Gord, the elder brother would not join us at prayer, but retired to another corner, his hands folded over his chest in defiance, while he glowered at his "parents" in resentment and hatred.

We who had organized the skit thought that we could slowly enact the rest of the story there in the chapel: the father running to meet and welcome the younger son, ordering the celebration, and then approaching the elder son in the courtyard. But Greg, as father, couldn't wait for Kathy and Timmy to decide to come home. As soon as he saw them he ran to the corner and embraced them and told them to come home. Meanwhile Karen, as mother, was over in the other corner trying to hug Gord and tell him that she wanted him to come into the home. It was over in less than a minute!

When our hearts are tuned in to peacemaking, we cannot tolerate the divisions between us. In the story of the Prodigal Son, the father goes out to meet both children, who are in disgrace and who have made themselves hateful by their actions. Jesus invites us to love that way and become people who make peace where there is division.

Bringing People Into the Heart of God

Write names and intentions on the cutout. Read them aloud and ask God's blessing on those named and all present. Attach the cutout to the backdrop, near the photograph for the week. End with the Lord's Prayer and a song.

Friday of the Third Week of Lent

*Gather in a circle and light a candle. Begin with the
following readings.*

The Beatitude

Wage peace—for your own heart and for the world in
which you live and move. In so doing, you tear open
the heavens, bringing love and truth into the midst of
violence and hatred.

The Word to Ponder

Sports is a passion for George. He keeps abreast of
the evolving lives of players and of teams by avidly
reading the sports newspapers and magazines every
day. At age seventy and with two hip replacements,
George has to live his sports vicariously. Daily he
reminds us of his meetings with a few of the celebrities
from Canadian football and baseball, as well as of the
fact that he "coaches" a hockey team in Scarborough.
In fact, the head coach of the team invites George into
the dressing room to talk to the players before and
during the games. It is the thrill of George's life.

Although sports violence was once something that
he took for granted and even enjoyed, George's
"coaching" has caused him to take a new position with
respect to fighting during a game. "You don't have to
fight to win! Pass the puck and stay out of the sin bin,"
he tells the players preparing for the game. "Play
hockey and play together! It doesn't matter who
scores the goal because everyone on the ice has a part
in the play."

George echoes the message of Jesus in the Gospel,
who continually encourages us to stay together, to
love one another and to live from the conviction that
each person offers us a gift to enrich our lives. If we
are bent on proving ourselves, on being better than
eveyone else, we live in a fighting mode. If, on the
other hand, we cooperate for peacemaking, we
energize our hearts. As George would say to his
hockey friends, "Play. Play together. Do your best.
Help one another to put the biscuit in the basket and

remember that you are a team!"

Write names and intentions on the cutout. Read them aloud and ask God's blessing on those named and all present. Attach the cutout to the backdrop, near the photograph for the week. End with the Lord's Prayer and a song.

Saturday of the Third Week of Lent

Gather in a circle and light a candle. Begin with the following readings.

The Beatitude

Work to make peace in your world and know that you grow more into the image of your Maker, who cherishes you as a beloved child.

The Word to Ponder

Every Wednesday the employees of The Woodery, the woodworking shop, gather the trash from several buildings on the farm property and unload it at the road for collection. Normally Ellen is not there because she has other responsibilities to share with Joe, the manager. One day when Joe was away, Ellen was assigned the trash detail, and she plunged in with a real desire to help. One of the regulars felt that Ellen was interfering and told her curtly to "Go home!"

Ellen's immediate response was anger, and she raised her fists to retaliate, forgetting in that instant that after she expresses her anger badly she suffers much grief. There was a tussle and energy was running high. Then, all of a sudden, Ellen stopped. After a pause she said, "I guess I should go home. I'm sorry, John." She reached out to shake John's hand and said, "I want to be your friend. Will you be my friend?"

Even when we are unable to control our first reaction to hurtful words or deeds, there is generally a moment to recover and choose again. By that time, it is embarrassing to shift gears, step over our bruised feelings and act from our desire for peace. To choose peace is to choose to feel better rather than worse about ourselves and others.

Bringing People Into the Heart of God

Write names and intentions on the cutout. Read them aloud and ask God's blessing on those named and all present. Attach the cutout to the backdrop, near the photograph for the week. End with the Lord's Prayer and a song.

The Fourth Week of Lent

The Merciful Will Obtain Mercy

Blessed are the merciful, for they will receive mercy.

The frightened child asks her parent to take her hand during a thunderstorm, or upon waking from a nightmare. A lover stretches a hand across the kitchen table after an argument, asking forgiveness for harsh words. A priest anoints the young man dying in the hospital bed, bathing the young man's forehead and hands in oils as he prays and calls upon God's mercy. Mercy is an intimate grace flowing beneath words, poured out in presence. It passes into our hearts through another's touch: hands holding ours, arms enfolding us, eyes looking deeply into us.

Jesus knew how to touch others with mercy. When he healed the sick he did so by touching them. He let Mary pour oils over his feet and dry them with her hair, even though it caused a scandal. When John, the beloved disciple, needed to feel loved, Jesus let him rest his head against his chest.

The last time Jesus sat with his friends for a meal, he knelt down and bathed their feet. Jesus touched each one of them in this way to teach them how to create community. Through his gestures, Jesus spoke to them of the intimacy and mercy at the heart of the new community that he wanted them to share.

Lent reminds us how badly we need this touch. Our lives are full of broken relationships and the scars left by anger and loss, disappointment and rejection. This week, we go beneath words and images and learn how to touch each other with respect and gentleness. The gift of God's mercy will flow over us as we hold each other and remember how to touch each other with mercy.

Sunday of the Fourth Week of Lent

Gather in a circle and light a candle. Begin with the following readings.

The Beatitude

When there is outward tension and division, try to build a bridge of peace. You have God's promise that the Spirit of Love will be with you and will help you to be an instrument of love.

The Word to Ponder

It had been a busy Saturday. People in the house were coming and going all day. Mary Bee realized that she was alone in the home to cook supper and be present with six core members. Frazzled, she asked the core members to help, and together they put the meal on the table and enjoyed the time together. After quiet time at the table, however, she "lost it" when she saw the kitchen, a disaster area of pots, pans and dirty dishes. She simply stood there, unable to cope, staring into space.

After a time, she heard herself saying aloud, "I really don't know what to do next." Dave H., who was also surveying the damage, extended his arms to encompass Mary Bee, Carol and Peter, saying, "I think that what we need now is a group hug!"

We can bring comfort to each other if we are tuned in to what others are experiencing. More important than any task is the peace that exists between us and the knowledge that we are loved, even when our performance is sometimes limited.

Bringing People Into the Heart of God

Write names and intentions on the cutout. Read them aloud and ask God's blessing on those named and all present. Attach the cutout to the backdrop, near the photograph for the week. End with the Lord's Prayer and a song.

Monday of the Fourth Week of Lent

Gather in a circle and light a candle. Begin with the following readings.

The Beatitude

Blessed are the merciful, for they will receive mercy.

The Word to Ponder

Carl had gone shopping to find four electric toothbrushes and after several attempts, had found only one in the whole town of Richmond Hill. As he went from one thing to another during a nonstop day, he became enraged at the lack of electric toothbrushes in Richmond Hill. While he realized that his feelings were getting the better of him, he was unable to cap the surges of blind fury. Then, just as people were sitting down to supper, one member of the household "had an accident" and left a huge mess in the bathroom, which Carl was unfortunate enough to discover. He cleaned it up, but he was in a state by the time he arrived at the table and sat down for supper. The table was noisy and he felt angry at the noise. His presence was less than comforting for those at the table who depend on him for good fun and good conversation! After some time Peter P. very quietly put his hand on Carl's. He patted him a few times, then said with great tenderness, "You're tired today, Carl."

When we feel critical toward the anger and behavior of another, we are encouraged by Jesus to tap the well of our kindness and care. In all his teachings Jesus urges us to love each other, to think kind thoughts and speak kind words. Mercy is to become the tent in which we dwell.

Bringing People Into the Heart of God

Write names and intentions on the cutout. Read them aloud and ask God's blessing on those named and all present. Attach the cutout to the backdrop, near the photograph for the week. End with the Lord's Prayer and a song.

Tuesday of the Fourth Week of Lent

*Gather in a circle and light a candle. Begin with the
following readings.*

The Beatitude

Blessed are you when you respond with compassion
to another in need. You will find yourself surrounded
by compassion.

The Word to Ponder

It was Heather's eighteenth birthday and time for the
party to begin. The house was decorated with
streamers and large paper musical notes dangling from
the ceiling because Heather is so fond of music. The
table held tasty treats of every description.

But Heather was having a difficult day. A warm
whirlpool bath just prior to the party did not relax
her. Heather, feeling anxious, was unable to stay with
us in the living room as guests began to arrive. Each
time someone helped her back to the living room and
to her rocking chair, Heather quietly got up and left
the room for the hallway, where she found solitude
and peace.

Heather's dad came, radiant with joy and bearing
gifts. When we pointed to the hallway, he disappeared.
The party began without the guest of honor, and we
sang, talked and began to enjoy the food. When
people left, they said it was a nice party, but each one
had missed the presence of Heather in our midst.

As we began to clear the dishes, we discovered the
real birthday party. Heather's father sat on the floor in
the hallway, holding Heather peacefully asleep on his
lap.

In Psalm 131 the psalmist describes God's tender
mercy in the words, "I have calmed and quieted my
soul,/like a weaned child with its mother" (Psalm
131:2). Our God, who shows us mercy, forgiveness
and love, wants us to share the comfort of that mercy
with each other.

Write names and intentions on the cutout. Read them aloud and ask God's blessing on those named and all present. Attach the cutout to the backdrop, near the photograph for the week. End with the Lord's Prayer and a song.

Wednesday of the Fourth Week of Lent

Gather in a circle and light a candle. Begin with the following readings.

The Beatitude

Shower mercy wherever you go. Your heart will learn compassion.

The Word to Ponder

Each Friday at noon, the workers in The Woodery go out together to the Richmond Hill Diner for lunch. This Friday ritual is a priority and seldom does anyone cancel. The workers are known and loved in the diner, and they relish this time, consuming burgers and fries and knowing that they will be late coming back for the afternoon.

Joe C., the director of The Woodery, was out of sorts one Friday, and the last thing he wanted to do was to go to the diner with the others for lunch. Feeling really down, he wanted to be alone. He felt sorry for himself and didn't want the noise or the camaraderie. Nevertheless, he decided that he would go, even though his reluctance showed in the way he slouched behind the wheel of the car.

David H. sat behind Joe and while they waited for the others to get in, David H. reached over and began to massage Joe's shoulders. When Joe became aware of what was happening, he said, "Dave, that feels wonderful. I'll give you a raise if you give me a good massage. It's just what I need right now!" Dave went on gently working his hands over Joe's shoulders and neck. Then he said, "I don't want a raise, Joe. I just want to be with you."

Jesus insists that we belong together, and that the Spirit of Love gives us words of comfort and healing to exchange with one another. Let us tune in to the moment today, seize it and be together with gentleness and compassion.

Write names and intentions on the cutout. Read them aloud and ask God's blessing on those named and all present. Attach the cutout to the backdrop, near the photograph for the week. End with the Lord's Prayer and a song.

Thursday of the Fourth Week of Lent

Gather in a circle and light a candle. Begin with the following readings.

The Beatitude

Happy are you when your heart is compassionate and merciful, for you yourself will receive compassion and mercy.

The Word to Ponder

Wendy and Peter R. had gone to the neighborhood furniture store, looking for some bedroom furniture. The employees were perfectly groomed, professional and distant. Taking a moment to relax, Wendy and Peter were sitting in the showroom chatting about their options when John, a member of Daybreak out for his evening walk, entered the store, oblivious to their presence.

John is slow of mind and especially of speech. He hasn't many words, but he has a great interest in and love for people. Wendy heard the girl at the desk say, "Oh, John, how are you tonight?" John answered, "Good!" and then asked, "You?" By the time she had answered, several of the employees who were not serving customers had gathered, all delighted to see John and spend a few minutes chatting with him. He asked one person, "Are you going to be home tonight?" and another, "How's your mom?" Then recognizing someone who had been on vacation, he said with great gusto, "Welcome back!" Whenever someone answered him, he generally said, "Oh, that's right!" as if he already knew the answer.

After only a few minutes he said his good-byes in order to continue his rounds of the shops in Richmond Hill. But Wendy and Peter said the employees continued talking and laughing together, somehow transformed by John's visit.

Jesus wants us to be as simple as doves. He wants our light to shine before all people. John points the way for us to recognize the many opportunities for gentle, human contact with the many people whom we

fail to recognize as brothers and sisters on the journey of life.

Bringing People Into the Heart of God

Write names and intentions on the cutout. Read them aloud and ask God's blessing on those named and all present. Attach the cutout to the backdrop, near the photograph for the week. End with the Lord's Prayer and a song.

Friday of the Fourth Week of Lent

Gather in a circle and light a candle. Begin with the following readings.

The Beatitude

Blessed are you when you show each other mercy.
You will live in an environment of care and love.

The Word to Ponder

Rosie is very small and only learned to walk at the age of twenty-five, having spent most of her life in a small crib in a nursing home. After ten years in her home in the community she now stands, and although she's unsteady, she walks about "as though she owns the place." Rosie has a history of broken relationships and doesn't trust people, usually keeping her distance. Without the ability to speak, she appears to love no one and to live apart from everyone who surrounds her.

Clara, one of the assistants, had a serious conflict with another assistant one day. She was visibly upset and crying. Trying to find a way to get hold of herself, she ducked into Rosie's room, closed the door and sat down on the bed. Sobbing into her hands, she wasn't immediately aware that Rosie had toddled into the room and had "caught" her in her grief. Clara began to wipe her eyes as Rosie, smiling and with determination, climbed onto the bed and plopped herself on Clara's lap, for the very first time in their eight months of living in the same house. Clara opened her arms to Rosie, who looked up, studying Clara's face with her eyes. Rosie's smile became a chuckle and then a laugh. The laughter tumbled out of her small, shaking body. Clara was unable to resist this clear invitation to be cared for by Rosie.

So often the spirit of mercy comes to us through unlikely givers. Small gestures of recognition, affirmation, love and forgiveness, given and received each day, are life and energy to keep us moving forward in our efforts to love and be loved. Let us open ourselves to give and receive mercy today.

Write names and intentions on the cutout. Read them aloud and ask God's blessing on those named and all present. Attach the cutout to the backdrop, near the photograph for the week. End with the Lord's Prayer and a song.

Saturday of the Fourth Week of Lent

*Gather in a circle and light a candle. Begin with the
following readings.*

The Beatitude

When you try to live from your deepest heart of
mercy, God rejoices in you.

The Word to Ponder

For a long time after moving to one of the Daybreak
homes, Anne Marie suffered the loss of her wonderful
family and circle of friends. For a long time, too, she
struggled to accept that although she was independent
in most areas of her life, having cerebral palsy made it
necessary for her to accept a certain amount of help
from assistants. Anne Marie would have preferred to
be totally independent and live on her own.

From the beginning, she became friends with
Carmen, who at that time lived in the home with her
husband, Steve, and their two children. The friendship
continued even when Steve and Carmen's family
decided to move to their own family home, and when
Carmen was no longer an assistant in the home. Anne
Marie and Carmen have been faithful to their
friendship for more than fifteen years. They have
shopped together, vacationed together, gone to
movies and brunches, and invited each other for
dinner on nights when they were cooking for their
respective households. They've shared in each other's
more intimate family times, too.

When Connie, Carmen's mother-in-law and dear
friend, was dying, Anne Marie consciously supported
Carmen through the difficult time. One day, toward
the end of Connie's life, Anne Marie called Carmen to
ask how she was doing. Carmen told Anne Marie that
it wouldn't be long until Connie died, and that she was
already anticipating how much she would miss Connie
when she was gone. Anne Marie, overcome with
sadness, said very simply, "Carm, I hope you know
that if I could, I would give my life for her." Without
waiting for a reply, she hung up the phone.

Compassion is a matter of the heart. Jesus talks about the people who produce treasures out of the goodness of their hearts. Today, each of us has the opportunity to speak and relate from the abundance of our hearts.

Bringing People Into the Heart of God

Write names and intentions on the cutout. Read them aloud and ask God's blessing on those named and all present. Attach the cutout to the backdrop, near the photograph for the week. End with the Lord's Prayer and a song.

The Pure in Heart
Will See God

Peter R., Elizabeth, Thelis

Blessed are the pure in heart, for they will see God.

Elizabeth has lived in L'Arche for over twenty years and played a leading role in many of our L'Arche communities worldwide. There's nothing she hasn't seen and nothing she won't tell you about. Her candor and her gritty Boston-Irish humor make her a natural storyteller. For years now, she has been our community "grandmother," carrying our history in her bones and reminding us of our joys and sorrows with her stories.

Imagine our surprise when Elizabeth asked the community to help her live as a hermit. With our help she set up her own small space in a quiet corner of our property near a beautiful wooded pond. Occasionally she visits with us, but most of her days are spent praying, working and reflecting in silence. It seems such an odd life for someone we know as a fiery spirit who relishes the busy life and the company of others.

But it is precisely this passionate love of life that calls Elizabeth to the quiet. She has roared into the silence to call upon God to break open her heart: not to find a peaceful retreat, but to enter into the very center of life's passion with new freedom.

The quiet is purifying her heart. Stillness burns away the myriad distractions and prayer teaches her to live life in the heart of God. Though she is quieter than before, she continues to tell her story; her fiery silence speaks of God's love more fiercely than her words ever did. As a solitary, Elizabeth is teaching us how to purify our hearts and dwell in God's presence. In the midst of a busy world, Elizabeth is showing us how to recognize the presence of a passionate and loving God dwelling in every moment.

Sunday of the Fifth Week of Lent

Gather in a circle and light a candle. Begin with the following readings.

The Beatitude

Blessed are the pure of heart, for they will see God.

The Word to Ponder

Riet came from Belgium to the Corner House two summers in a row, particularly to help Tracy, Alia and Heather, none of whom speak and all of whom have very special needs. Eighteen months after her final summer, Riet wrote back to the home:

"Why, since I left, do I feel unfulfilled? It has to do with each of you and with Alia.... In the Corner House I found a well to quench my thirst.... And there was Alia, who was my first friend at Daybreak and the person who led me to that well. Long after I was back I felt that she had the power to bring me to my own deepest core. Alia, so silent and so dependent, not only revealed to me my power to love, but also my weak sides. More than that, she told me in her own way and without any words that there is no need to be afraid, that we are never alone if we have faith. This created a very strong bond between us so that coming home was hard. I felt I had left myself behind. I tried hard to overcome this disturbing feeling and to continue my way here in Belgium, but I still feel cut off. No one has come that close to me ever since leaving. Here, I seem to have no time to sit with someone quietly, as I did when I shared time with Alia. I miss the silence. I think our God is a God of silence. I miss Alia."

Our inner attitude toward weaker people draws us to care, but not to expect any return. From a spiritual perspective we minister to each other when we share our gifts. We readily recognize the gifts and skills of organization many of us offer to others, but the seemingly poorer people among us, by their

dependency and need for presence, offer us the invaluable opportunity to visit and welcome the deep and often hidden places of our souls.

Today, open yourself to receive something of value from someone who depends on you.

Bringing People Into the Heart of God

Write names and intentions on the cutout. Read them aloud and ask God's blessing on those named and all present. Attach the cutout to the backdrop, near the photograph for the week. End with the Lord's Prayer and a song.

Monday of the Fifth Week of Lent

Gather in a circle and light a candle. Begin with the following readings.

The Beatitude

A little child is pure of heart. Jesus invites us to let the little child in us shine in our relationships with one another.

The Word to Ponder

The more people Suzanne can manage to see and visit with in one day, the happier she is. She very often approaches her friends with the question, "When can you and I get together for lunch?" When they do get together, Suzanne loves to tell stories about when she was a little girl. Then she asks her friend, "What were you like when you were a child? Who did you play with? Tell me more stories about your childhood." Then she adds, "Would you like to see my special album, with all my baby pictures, and with some of the people who were close to me when I was a child?" With great delight she points to those who were so significant for her and who bring her joy even to this day.

Sometimes Suzanne has difficulty staying in reality. She also has a hearing loss that excludes her from those experiences she most wants to share. Her life is not easy, yet she makes enormous efforts to overcome her anxiety and rise to the occasion. Suzanne reveled in the joy of her birthday party, when all her friends brought their baby pictures and she had to try to guess who was who. Suzanne, by effort and love, calls forth and welcomes the inner child in the people that she meets.

Jesus told us that we must "become like little children," safe in God's unending love for us. Knowing we are loved frees us to love another, even if that person is sometimes difficult. We need to make the effort to live from this belief.

Bringing People Into the Heart of God

Write names and intentions on the cutout. Read them aloud and ask God's blessing on those named and all present. Attach the cutout to the backdrop, near the photograph for the week. End with the Lord's Prayer and a song.

Tuesday of the Fifth Week of Lent

Gather in a circle and light a candle. Begin with the following readings.

The Beatitude

Those who live from the well of love in the center of their hearts see God in a special way.

The Word to Ponder

Linda's deepest gift is her power to make people feel welcome and special. When people visit, Linda walks right up to them, extends her hand in welcome, exchanges names, takes their coats and invites them to be "at home." Because there are many, many visitors, we sometimes wonder how Linda sustains the authentic character of her welcome.

In her bedroom, Linda has fashioned a prayer corner. She has a cross, an icon and photos of those who are close to her, all positioned on a beautiful cloth in a tiny space in the corner of the small room. When Linda changed bedrooms not long ago, she wasted no time in arranging her prayer corner in the new space.

Just before bedtime, Linda often invites someone in the house to pray with her. They sit together in the prayer corner, and Linda prays for each of her friends pictured there, as well as for people she has heard of who need prayers. Then she invites her guest to pray. The invitation into Linda's prayer time and space is really an invitation into Linda's heart. There, one is treated to a vision of faithfulness given out of love.

Today, in the joy and the pain of our personal relationships, we can always pray for each other and carry one another in our hearts.

Bringing People Into the Heart of God

Write names and intentions on the cutout. Read them aloud and ask God's blessing on those named and all present. Attach the cutout to the backdrop, near the photograph for the week. End with the Lord's Prayer and a song.

Wednesday of the Fifth Week of Lent

Gather in a circle and light a candle. Begin with the following readings.

The Beatitude

The pure of heart see where God is to be found.

The Word to Ponder

Ian is attracted to people in need. His prayer is often for the poor, for someone who has recently fallen ill or for the victims of disasters reported in the news. He seems to notice those in difficulty, and he remembers, day after day, to pray for them. People in his home say that Ian continually reminds them to bring those who are less fortunate into their prayer, asking always for God's mercy.

The people of the house were planning a games night, and Cheryl suggested that all those invited should be asked to pay one dollar. "Then," she joked, "we could buy something really nice for our house!" Ian was not amused and answered with conviction, "But we really don't need anything. Besides, the only way that I would collect money from people is in order to do something for the people who are poor."

Jesus, too, identified with people who were rejected, suffering and poor. We have yet to learn that God is hiding in those who are in need, waiting to meet us and call forth the wells of compassion that would otherwise stagnate within us.

Bringing People Into the Heart of God

Write names and intentions on the cutout. Read them aloud and ask God's blessing on those named and all present. Attach the cutout to the backdrop, near the photograph for the week. End with the Lord's Prayer and a song.

Thursday of the Fifth Week of Lent

Gather in a circle and light a candle. Begin with the following readings.

The Beatitude

Happy are those whose hearts are pure. They understand what others fail to see.

The Word to Ponder

During a house meeting, the people of the home were talking about the line in our charter that says, "Each person is of unique and sacred value, and each one has the same dignity and the same rights." Marg asked, "What does that mean?" Kathy replied, "It means, Marg, that you are special." Cheryl went on to say, "Unique means that there is only one you, that there is no one in the whole world like you, and that you, Marg, are a very special and beautiful person. Did you know that?" Marg looked directly at Cheryl and quietly answered, "Yes, I know." Then after a pause she said, "Thank you."

Each person in our family, our school, our work has a unique and mysterious value that we often do not see. Each of us also has an unrepeatable gift of life and love. Through the prophet Isaiah, God speaks to you and me: "Do not be afraid.... / I have called you, you are mine.... /...you are precious in my sight, and honored, and I love you" (Isaiah 43:1, 4). Can we, like Marg, hear this word? Can we also say, "Yes, I know it is true. Thank you, God"?

Bringing People Into the Heart of God

Write names and intentions on the cutout. Read them aloud and ask God's blessing on those named and all present. Attach the cutout to the backdrop, near the photograph for the week. End with the Lord's Prayer and a song.

Friday of the Fifth Week of Lent

*Gather in a circle and light a candle. Begin with the
following readings.*

The Beatitude

Those whose hearts are pure "see" the presence of
the loving God in our midst.

The Word to Ponder

Mary and Joe's wedding was like a "family" weekend.
Both come from large families who have large families.
Everyone came! Besides the families, both Mary and
Joe had been members of the Daybreak community,
and the hundred community members who were
invited came, too! It was a wonderful celebration!

David H., a Daybreak core member and Joe's best
friend, was the best man. Joe had called David first to
tell him of their engagement so that David could
"scoop" the news to the whole community. At the
wedding, David overcame his restlessness to be
incredibly attentive to Joe, and to hold himself present
to the liturgy and to the wedding ceremony. He took
his place in the reception line, but after a short time he
was unable to stay with it, so he disappeared to smoke
his pipe.

Mel, another Daybreak core member and friend of
Joe and Mary's, saw David disappear. He knew that
David couldn't manage it all, but he also knew that
David's absence left a hole in the reception line.
Without hesitating, Mel stepped into David's place and
began to welcome the guests, ask their names,
introduce himself as friend of Joe and Mary, and thank
them for coming to the wedding. When Mary looked
down the line and saw him, she felt grateful for Mel's
overflowing love and gesture of concern.

Sometimes we offer love as we offer eyedrops out
of an eyedropper, one drop at a time, but the
Scriptures call us to open the floodgates within and to
let our love overflow, available to all people and
situations. Perhaps we must ask ourselves why we
hesitate to step into situations where the need for

love is obvious. Why are we so afraid that we may be misunderstood? Jesus calls us to look with eyes of care, to listen with sensitivity and to respond with gestures of love.

Bringing People Into the Heart of God

Write names and intentions on the cutout. Read them aloud and ask God's blessing on those named and all present. Attach the cutout to the backdrop, near the photograph for the week. End with the Lord's Prayer and a song.

Saturday of the Fifth Week of Lent

*Gather in a circle and light a candle. Begin with the
following readings.*

The Beatitude

Uncontrolled anger, resentment, criticism, lust and
jealousy are attitudes that cause our hearts to be
polluted and sick. Forgiveness, kindness, caring,
respect, listening and welcoming provide space and
"vision" to recognize God's spirit of love bonding us
together with hope.

The Word to Ponder

Annie, Helen F. and Jane live together in apartment
#612. It is small, sometimes too small for the women
to find enough personal space. They share the same
spirit and the same desire to live in community, but
often their differences take an upper hand. Helen says
her experience of life with Annie and Jane is like
attending a school of the Scriptures. "Jane is my
teacher," she says, "and I never cease to wonder at
her unending ability to forgive and begin with me
again. Some days, when we have had to try to forgive
each other seventy times seven times, Jane will look
up at me from her bed as I set her alarm, and with her
wonderful toothless smile she will say, 'Hallie, I'ze
sorry.... I like you.' And she gives me a big hug. Just as
I leave the room, though, to hold me in the reality of
our relationship, she calls after me, 'Turkey!' "

The challenge of the gospel is the challenge to stay
in love. Relationships will be messy and difficult, but
Jesus asks us to find the support and the means to
forgive and forgive and forgive, not waiting for the
other to respond or to change. How do we find these
supports? By calling on the Spirit to fill our hearts with
divine love, by looking at the other with God's eyes
and listening with God's ears, by guarding our hearts
from being filled with darkness, anger and resentment.

Write names and intentions on the cutout. Read them aloud and ask God's blessing on those named and all present. Attach the cutout to the backdrop, near the photograph for the week. End with the Lord's Prayer and a song.

The Persecuted Receive the Kingdom

Bill, Peter P.

Blessed are those who are persecuted for righteousness' sake, for theirs is the kingdom of heaven.

Peter P. never talks about the institution. The memory of that life and of some of the things he experienced there torments him, especially when he is afraid or tired.

Bill doesn't like to talk about his illness. He gets frightened when he falls down, when he has to use his oxygen mask, when he has to face the fact that he may die soon.

These feelings visit Peter and Bill like a persecution: a time of pain and terror. Persecution comes to each of us. When we are alone, tired and vulnerable, the darkness washes over us.

The wonderful thing is that Bill and Peter have found a hope to get them through the darkness. When Peter puts his feet up on the couch and Bill gets after him, bugging him and teasing him, it takes away the darkness. Sitting together, they are safe. Their friendship reveals the hope of a warm home, a safe place in which to ride out the terrors of the nighttime.

This is what Jesus was speaking of when he taught about the kingdom of heaven. It was a way of describing friendship as a refuge from fear. Friendship is a safe place in which we taste the promise of heaven. Though the fears will come back, just as they do for Peter and Bill, they will not overpower us. Through friendship we learn to calm our fears and quiet the terror. When the darkness comes, we know that someone is there to hold us until it passes.

Palm Sunday

Gather in a circle and light a candle. Begin with the following readings.

The Beatitude

Blessed are those who are persecuted for righteousness' sake, for theirs is the kingdom of heaven.

The Word to Ponder

Occasionally one of us recognizes that look of pain on Lloyd's face. None of us knows very well the things that he has lived and lost in his life, but we sense that there has been great loss. For fifty years Lloyd lived with his family and proudly worked the holstein farm with his dad. The sign read, "J. Kerman and Son." When J. Kerman died, Lloyd lost his place on the farm. Later, he lost his dog. When his mother died and the farm was sold, Lloyd lost his home. Coming to live in Daybreak meant that Lloyd lost some of the intimacy that he had enjoyed with his family. Of late he has needed more help with his personal care and especially with his bath, so he has lost some of his independence.

Just below Lloyd's grief, though, is a deep well of humor. We have only to hint that jersey cows are better than holsteins, and Lloyd's face will crinkle up in a huge smile and he will yell, "No way!" People rub it in when they see Lloyd wearing his holstein T-shirts, caps and sweaters! He has been given holstein mugs, calendars and throw rugs. Just mention jerseys and he crinkles up his face and offers the same response: "No way!" He loves to tease others in the same way we tease him about cows. Lloyd, in his own way, instructs us in the art of living with loss.

Jesus teaches us always to trust. Do not worry, relax together, calm down, he instructs us, because our loving God knows all our needs.

Write names and intentions on the cutout. Read them aloud and ask God's blessing on those named and all present. Attach the cutout to the backdrop, near the photograph for the week. End with the Lord's Prayer and a song.

Monday of Holy Week

Gather in a circle and light a candle. Begin with the following readings.

The Beatitude

In your life as a follower of Jesus, you will suffer. Try to believe that your suffering, linked to Christ's, has a mysterious meaning that has to do with the Kingdom of God and salvation.

The Word to Ponder

Helen H. loved her independence. With great earnestness, she told the bus driver that we had taken her money, so he let her ride free. Then she went off to have coffee at the local restaurant! She refused to come out of her room for the fire drill because she didn't like the noise, and she hated to be hurried! She locked herself in the bathroom when it was her turn to set the table, and she'd disappear if we mentioned that we were going to celebrate her birthday with a party. Helen was so alive and full of creativity!

Today Helen is in the final stages of Alzheimer's disease and resides in the long-term care wing of the local hospital. Her personality has changed and her spunk is gone. A few weeks ago, we were called because Helen was having difficulty breathing, and we thought she would die. In her final months and weeks Helen is, perhaps, the poorest person in our community. She is very beautiful and precious, and she is a silent teacher on the subject of life and death. She is peaceful and as comfortable as she can be. She has many, many visitors who love her and who go faithfully to cheer her along her passage into eternity.

Life is too short to hold a grudge, too short to be possessed by anger over the aggravations that are surely present among those who live together. The seeds of death are at work in each one of us. Our lives, our strengths and our sufferings have meaning in the eyes of the God who loves us, who lived and put great energy into loving, who suffered and who gave his life as a ransom for us.

Bringing People Into the Heart of God

Write names and intentions on the cutout. Read them aloud and ask God's blessing on those named and all present. Attach the cutout to the backdrop, near the photograph for the week. End with the Lord's Prayer and a song.

Tuesday of Holy Week

Gather in a circle and light a candle. Begin with the following readings.

The Beatitude

At his baptism Jesus heard the voice of God calling him "Beloved Son." Even as the beloved of God, Jesus suffered terribly. We, who suffer in our lives, are also beloved sons and daughters of God. We belong to the Kingdom of God.

The Word to Ponder

Mike R., like so many other people in the world, has experienced serious losses over which he had no control. The gradual loss of his sight has been frustrating and distressing. A sensitive man, Mike has sometimes been unable to cope and his feelings of frustration and anger come out in words. Whenever this happens, Mike knows it and it adds to his pain. The true beauty of Mike's personality is reflected in his relationships, especially with his family. He is deeply attached to them. He also has a "mate," Sean, and these two bring out the best in each other.

Camping with Sean, Mike is totally himself. On the way, they divide the cost of the supplies, but Mike has to cajole Sean into giving over his share of "smackeroos" (their nickname for money). Together, they raise the tent, and Mike has to stand underneath it in the center and raise it up just right. With Sean's help he roasts marshmallows and even drives the boat. They exchange stories around the campfire, and each time Sean talks about his daughter and some of the things she's doing, Mike asks delightedly, "So, did you ground her, Sean?"

Says Sean, "Mike probably knows more about me and my family than anyone else. He's one of my best friends!"

Jesus was able to live his sufferings, knowing that he was loved, that God was with him. In this Holy Week he invites us not to get rid of our grief, but to trust that it can shape us into compassionate people.

Write names and intentions on the cutout. Read them aloud and ask God's blessing on those named and all present. Attach the cutout to the backdrop, near the photograph for the week. End with the Lord's Prayer and a song.

The Poor in Spirit Receive the Kingdom

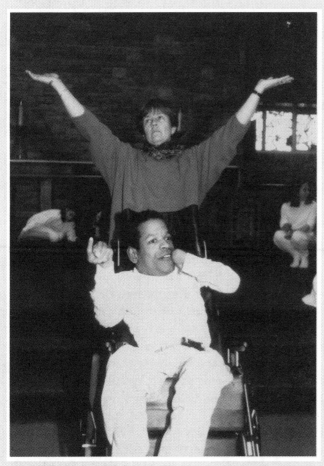

Michael B., Stephanie

Blessed are the poor in spirit, for theirs is the kingdom of heaven.

When people first meet Michael B., they often see his wheelchair before they see him. They hear the screams he makes as his body, overcome with excitement, goes into spasms. His behavior often makes it difficult to carry on a conversation. Michael can't always get his point across, and others sometimes mistake his inability to communicate for an inability to understand. Though people begin talking *to* Michael, they quickly begin talking *about* him with one of his friends. It is so painful to be with Michael when this happens and to see all his enthusiasm and openness go unanswered. He has so much to share, but it seems so impossible for others to understand—except when Michael dances.

As part of the Spirit Movers dance troupe, Michael is able to share his spirit with others. Though he is still in the same chair, still unable to use words, with the help of the other performers, Michael is transformed. His body relaxes, his eyes shine with joy, and he shares a radiant smile as he moves through the rhythm of the dance. Every gesture that he makes, every movement of his eyes is full of grace and meaning. When Michael dances, his spirit is set free and he can share his story.

And people understand. More than that, they begin to weep as they recognize that Michael is reaching into their own hearts and telling their stories through his movements. On the deepest level, spirit speaks to spirit and a new word is spoken. Where people saw only struggle and poverty they discover remarkable beauty and grace. This ability to reveal the promise of joy and beauty hidden within a struggling heart is Michael's precious gift.

Wednesday of Holy Week

*Gather in a circle and light a candle. Begin with the
following readings.*

The Beatitude

Blessed are the poor in spirit, for theirs is the kingdom
of heaven.

The Word to Ponder

Gord H. knows the Lord as he knows a friend. He
talks to God with great confidence and faith and he
receives God's word directly into his heart.
Sometimes the word may be too complicated for his
mind to understand, but he seizes it with his heart and
says to the homilist after the service, "Oh, that was so
good. It touched me in my heart."

In our morning prayer service we announce our
intentions. No one takes longer than thirty seconds to
say the names of those for whom they wish to pray.
No one, that is, except Gord! He begins slowly, "I'd
like to pray for Ben. Ben is such a good man, and my
friend. I hope Ben is OK. And I pray for Henri. I miss
Henri when he is away. Give Henri the strength."
Now Gord is warming up, and he continues, "And I
pray for Mary Bee who is trying to make a decision
about going to India or staying in Daybreak. Give Mary
Bee the strength. I pray for Thelis, who broke her
knee. Give Thelis the strength. I'd like to pray for Joe,
who is my boss in The Woodery. Give Joe and his wife,
Kathy, the strength. Let's pray for my buddy Bill, who
has a sore leg. Give Bill the strength. And I pray for my
mudder. She is such a good mudder. I love my mudder.
Give her the strength. And give strength to my family;
my brother Ian, my brother Brian and his wife,
Paulette, and for Joan, my sister, and Paul and the
children." Gord may then pause before winding up
with, "And I give thanks to you, God, for Helen. Helen
is in the hospital and is sick. I pray for Helen, and I ask
you, God, to give Helen the strength. Let us pray to
the Lord."

Perhaps, when I hear myself saying, "I cannot pray,"

95

I need to become more simple and straightforward. Prayer is the voice of the child within, announcing the deepest yearnings of the heart. Today, listen with your heart to the encounter between Jesus and Bartimaeus. Jesus asks him, "What would you like me to do for you?" and he replies, "Lord, that I may see" (Mark 10:51). Prayer is an encounter with Love.

Bringing People Into the Heart of God

Write names and intentions on the cutout. Read them aloud and ask God's blessing on those named and all present. Attach the cutout to the backdrop, near the photograph for the week. End with the Lord's Prayer and a song.

Holy Thursday

*Gather in a circle and light a candle. Begin with the
following readings.*

The Beatitude

Blessed are the poor in spirit, for theirs is the kingdom
of heaven.

The Word to Ponder

Year after year, day after day, hour after hour, Adam
radiates peace. Peace is his gift to those who care for
him and to those who love him. Adam's life is like a
peace offering, for he asks very little and he gives
abundantly. Adam sits in his chair or lies on his bed. He
does not walk unless there is someone behind him,
supporting him. Adam listens but cannot speak. He
loves his dinner and can feed himself with minimal
help. Large doses of medication cannot prevent his
having many seizures every day, and this can be very
tiring. Waiting for someone to attend to his intimate
needs is wearing. Watching but having no voice is
difficult. Being robbed of independence is not easy or
fun. It seems that Adam, in the depths of his heart, has
accepted his life as it is being offered to him. And from
those depths a radiance and a peace are offered to the
world.

There is a privileged place within each of us where
we choose our responses to our pain. Jesus
encourages us to believe that he is there, with us,
offering us all the courage, the strength and the love
that we need to become people of peace and even joy.

Bringing People Into the Heart of God

*Write names and intentions on the cutout. Read them
aloud and ask God's blessing on those named and all
present. Attach the cutout to the backdrop, near the
photograph for the week. End with the Lord's Prayer and a
song.*

Good Friday

Gather in a circle and light a candle. Begin with the following readings.

The Beatitude

When your heart is clear, you are blessed and you radiate the Kingdom of God that is within you.

The Word to Ponder

A rather nervous man, Francis acts quickly and sometimes appears to be angry and defensive. Perhaps he is angry and disturbed because he can remember that he was laughed at when he was small and lived in a small town. Somewhere inside himself he knew or was made to feel that he could not quite keep up in his large family and in his school. Somewhere he received a strong message that he was different from the others.

Yet Francis is the first to greet guests who come to his home. With a firm handshake, he announces, "I'm Francis. Would you like to see our house?" After showing people around, he proudly pulls out his "Lifestory" book containing photos of his childhood and his life in Daybreak, as well as letters from people in his hometown who responded to his letters asking them to tell him what they remembered about him. He excitedly explains who each person is and describes the places that have been so dear to his heart. For last year's Lenten reflection Francis wrote, "God watches over me wherever I go. God helps me in what I do. God helps me pray and gives me friends."

Today we commemorate the death of Jesus on the cross. Although he suffered enormously, Jesus died with great dignity, accepting his death as he had accepted his life. He was not angry in death, though he had reason to be, and in his final hour, he let his enemies go free. With the Spirit that he sent us, we can do likewise, finding our true identity as God's beloved daughters and sons.

Write names and intentions on the cutout. Read them aloud and ask God's blessing on those named and all present. Attach the cutout to the backdrop, near the photograph for the week. End with the Lord's Prayer and a song.

Francis

Holy Saturday

Gather in a circle and light a candle. Begin with the following readings.

The Beatitude

There is a beautiful kingdom for those whose hearts are clear.

The Word to Ponder

John B. is an extrovert. His energy surges in large groups, and his enthusiasm overflows whenever we are in the midst of a project. John also loves women and in his efforts to relate, has sometimes gone a bit overboard. One day a young lady came for supper to his home and he found her very attractive, so he made certain that he sat next to her at the table and accompanied her everywhere she went during her brief visit. She got in her car to leave, and was speaking to one of the assistants through the driver-side window, when John approached and leaned through the passenger-side window to bid her farewell. Because of his difficulty with speech, the assistant interpreted his one word question "Help?" by adding, "John is asking if there is anything he can do to help you before you go." Somewhat flustered the young woman replied, "Oh, OK, yes, John, you could just pull out my aerial, thank you." John pulled himself out of the window, grasped the aerial in his hand, pulled it right out of its socket and handed it to his shocked friend through the open window of the car! Without blinking, the young woman caringly thanked John, allowing him to feel appreciated for his overflowing goodness.

When there is no one to interpret, John's efforts to love are often frustrated and he is very often misunderstood. His beautiful and caring heart has been offended by rejection. He waits patiently for a look of appreciation in response to the kindnesses that he offers with such tender care.

The disciples did not understand and their hearts were broken. On Saturday, they lived the pain of the loss of Jesus. They waited, not knowing what to do next. They were soon to discover how close God is to the brokenhearted.

Bringing People Into the Heart of God

Write names and intentions on the cutout. Read them aloud and ask God's blessing on those named and all present. Attach the cutout to the backdrop, near the photograph for the week. End with the Lord's Prayer and a song.

Easter Sunday

Gather in a circle and light a candle. Begin with the following readings.

The Beatitude

The poor are the treasure of the Church! They live in God's kingdom.

The Word to Ponder

When she first came to live at Daybreak, Helen J. seemed unable to decide whether she wanted people to be close or distant. Consistently and without looking at you, she'd take your hand, pulling you toward her. Just as you imagined that you were being

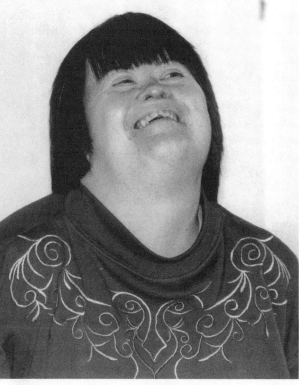

Helen J.

welcomed by her, she'd push you away! Without speaking or looking, Helen communicated articulately with pull and push for about three years. Gradually, the pull and push declined, and Helen began to look. One day she smiled! Now she laughs and sings. One day at worship, Doug instructed the congregation to look at Helen and follow her lead for the song "I Will Sing, I Will Sing, a Song Unto the Lord." As he played, Helen began clapping her hands, so everyone began to clap. Then she opened her mouth and the sounds came forth. Finally, as the pace of the hymn increased, she threw her head back, laughing and praising, "Alleluia, Glory to the Lord." Each one in the group, following her lead, did likewise.

When I feel loved or when I love another, my spirit comes alive. Jesus rose from the dead and gave us his spirit of love. This spirit is available to us so that we can experience the Kingdom, and the Resurrection, even before we die.

Bringing People Into the Heart of God

Write names and intentions on the cutout. Read them aloud and ask God's blessing on those named and all present. Attach the cutout to the backdrop, near the photograph for the week. End with the Lord's Prayer and a song.

Patterns for Cutouts